The Official BEANIE BASHER Handbook

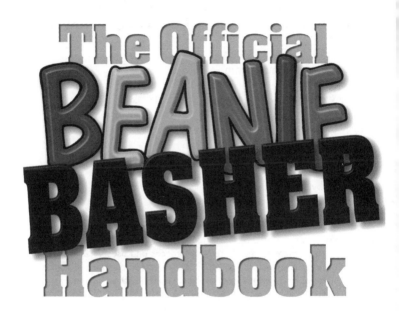

The Official BEANIE BASHER Handbook

by "Dr." B. Neebascher

Andrews McMeel
Publishing

Kansas City

www.andrewsmcmeel.com

98 99 00 01 02 RDC 10 9 8 7 6 5 4 3 2 1

ISBN: 0-8362-8186-1

Library of Congress Catalog Card Number: 98-86600

ATTENTION: SCHOOLS AND BUSINESSES

Andrews McMeel books are available at quantity discounts with
bulk purchase for educational, business, or sales promotional use.
For information, please write to: Special Sales Department,
Andrews McMeel Publishing, 4520 Main Street, Kansas City,
Missouri 64111.

Contents

Introduction
What's the Big Deal about Beanies?

•••••••••••••••••••••••••••••••

Since 1993, people worldwide have been buying little plush stuffed animals by the millions! The most popular of these stuffed toys are Beanie Babies® brought to you by Ty, Inc., Oak Brook, Illinois. Each of the over one hundred Beanies (at the time of this printing) is produced in quantities of up to 10,000,000. Beanies outsell Barbie dolls! Ty indeed has become the McDonald's of the plush toy world. (McDonald's Corporation is also located in Oak Brook, Illinois, and, by the way, just purchased 240 million Teenie-Beanies™, which they intend to sell within a month.)

I have personally witnessed the horror of women actually at each other's throats grabbing for these limp little critters as soon as Beanies reach the retail bins. Why? Is there something in these Beanies that they are after? Do they really think Beanies are that cute? Or do they believe that plush and beans will be the next world currency?

This book discusses the finer points of Beaniedom and uncovers findings that, without the diligence of our team of crack researchers and the selfless desire of our publisher to bring to light their startling discoveries, might have been found only in the pages of the *National Enquirer*.

It is our sincere desire that our findings can save just one person from financial ruin, or at the very least, deter a full-fledged alien invasion.

–"Dr." B. Neebascher   (*pronouned* **Knee**-*Basher*)
July 1998

Note: No Beanies were harmed in the production of this book. (We waited until the book was written, printed, bound, and in the stores—then we ran over the entire lot with a steamroller, set them on fire, and tilled their ashes into our compost pile.)

Chapter One
The Evolution
of Beanies

● ●

"I'm sure that this is one evolution that neither God nor Darwin would like to be associated with."

They didn't always have legs.

I remember in kindergarten there was a big clown face painted on a piece of masonite (a hard piece of plywoodlike material–minus the plys–invented by the Masons shortly after they invented jars). The clown's face had round holes cut in its eyes, nose, and mouth areas through which we tossed small cloth bags filled with dried beans for various point values. We called these little bean–filled cloth bags "beanbags."

Figure 1
1950s vintage beanbag and clown face.

(artist's rendering)

They grew to fill our rooms.

In the '60s, these little beanbags grew in size and found their way into our family rooms and dorm rooms as chairs. We called them beanbag chairs. Having accidentally ripped a few open, I can report that the beans had been replaced by Styrofoam beads (possibly originated by the dried-bean shortage of 1962). Thankfully, the clown face didn't also grow in size.

*Figure b
1960s vintage
beanbag chair in
use by a hippie.*

(artist's rendering)

They shrank and bounced on knees.

In the '70s, the beanbags shrank to near their original size and formed a ball–like shape. They were immediately embraced by the youth of the '70s and '80s who stood in circles bouncing the beanbag balls off their knees to one another. The beanbag balls became known as Hacky Sacks (most likely because they resembled a huge fur–ball that a cat would *hack* up).

*Figure III
1970s and 80s
beanbag ball
game called
Hacky Sack.*

(not actual photo)

They grew legs.

The 1980s weren't that good for any of us. The nuclear power plant leaks of the late '70s/early '80s had left their glowing residue on both the United States and Russia. Since beanbags aren't living creatures, we doubt that the radiation leaks from these plants had anything to do with the development of legs on beanbags. However, the radiation may have affected the manual dexterity of the seamstresses that were sewing them, resulting in beanbag bulges that, oddly enough, resembled legs.

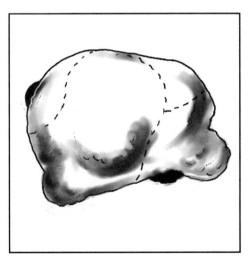

Figure 4
1980s beanbag.

(artist's rendering)

They grew into a profit center.

We have surmised that shortly before the dawn of 1993, a guy stumbled upon some of these mutant beanbags and recognized their potential.* In 1993 a series of nine plush bean-filled animals–complete with legs, tails, and heads–emerged on the retail market. A tribute to good old American ingenuity and deft marketing, Beanies have now touched almost every family in America and can be found in the most remote corners of the globe.

*This is entirely speculation on our part.

*Figure five
A 1990s generic
Beanie animal
toy.*

(stick drawing)

Guest Editorial by Dale Connelly
The Hunt

● ●

The kids who collect Beanies will be all right. It's the adults who are frightening. The hardened adult Beanie collector drives a minivan so packed with spoils that they need trailer mirrors so they can see what's behind them. They speed into parking lots, park across two spaces, throw open the door with the engine still knocking, and stride up to the counter to say, "You got any of them monkey dolls? All I need is that one and that cat." And somewhere deep inside there's a tiny voice that says, "This is sick. You're twisted. You sap, why did you fall for this?"

There is a reason, and I think it's ancient. It's the hunt. The prehistoric urge to track something down and bag it before someone else does, so that you and yours can eat and propagate. Most people don't do that anymore—we've become softened by consumerism; we can buy what we need. But now these big corporations have found a way to tap the compulsion, to tie marketing to survival and re-create the hunt.

That's why the beanbags are shaped like animals. That's why otherwise reasonable adults find themselves milling around by the condiment counter mumbling things like, "I heard they had Doby at the Shop 'N' Save." It's the thrill of victory. The seduction of the chase.

If it weren't for this we might be out in the woods, waiting for deer. *That* would be dangerous.

—Dale Connelly is the cohost of The Morning Show *on Minnesota Public Radio.*

Chapter Two
Beanie Anatomy 101

● ●

CAUTION:
This chapter contains unretouched
photographs of an actual
Beanie autopsy.

It is *not* for the squeamish.

You have been warned.

Above: Our Beanie autopsy specimen prior to the autopsy.

Beanie Autopsy

● ●

I had to know.

Since the beanbag I remembered from kindergarten was filled with dried beans, beanbag
chairs with Styrofoam beads, and Hacky Sacks
with little pealike things, I just had to know
what was in those little stuffed plush toys. So,
sparing no expense, I hired the best veterinary
surgeon I could find for $5 and a bottle of cold
beer. I'll call him *Dr. Al* (he wishes to remain
anonymous). Dr. Al proceeded to instruct me in
the finer points of Beanie dissection that he
learned in his high school biology class.
Apparently, Dr. Al is still working on his degree
in veterinary medicine at night school. (His day
job has something to do with car repair or sep-
tic tank vacuuming or something.)

The proper tool selection

The selection of the right tools for the job is as important in Beanie autopsies as it is when you are plumbing your basement bathroom. We know. Dr. Al said so.

Listed below are Dr. Al's selection of tools for the Beanie autopsy (also pictured on the right).

1. C–clamp
2. Utility knife
3. X–Acto knife
4. Tin snips
5. Scissors
6. Hacksaw
7. Pipe–cutter thing
8. Gas mask
9. Vise–Grips
10. Wire cutter (a.k.a. diagonal sheers)
11. Duct tape

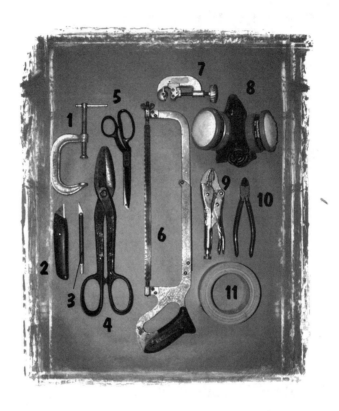

Above: Tools recommended by Dr. Al for Beanie autopsies. We included the gas mask just in case the stuff inside was of a hazardous nature. We found out later this was an unnecessary precaution—at least at this time (see Conspiracy Theories, chapter 3).

The initial incision

A sharp razor blade or X–Acto knife will do nicely if you don't have a scalpel. The utility knife shown on the right of the Beanie may tend to rip the fabric and cut your coffee table. If you choose the razor blade option, please use a single-edge blade as found in paint and hardware stores, *not* a double edge or injector blade. The double edge will tend to dissect your fingers as well as the Beanie, and the injector blade will just make you look silly. (Please note: There is no need to shave the Beanie before you make your incision.)

Step #1: Cut through the belly of the Beanie in a straight line (usually identifiable by a seam) from the neck to the tail of the Beanie. A slight sawing motion will aid you in your incision. You should not be cutting all the way through to the back of the Beanie (we will get to this in chapter 5: Retiring Your Own Beanies).

Above: The dotted line represents the approximate location and length of your first incision.

Spilling the beans about NO beans!

We were shocked to find little white beads, or pelletlike things, in the torso of the Beanie and a lot of fuzzy stuff in the head, legs, and tail. There were no beans in sight! Not one! Not dried, not green, not jelly–*no beans!*

Above: All of the stuff we found inside.

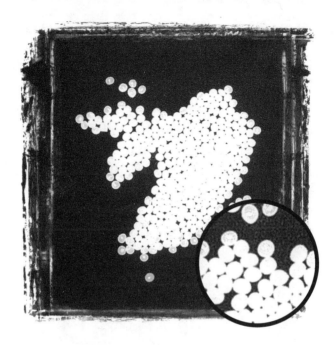

The beads didn't resemble anything that we've ever seen before. We are still concerned about what they actually are *(see chapter 3)*.

Maybe a little truth in advertising is in order here. Call these toys what they are: *Pelletlike Thing Babies!*

Above: The mysterious white beads found in the torso and a 2X magnification of the same.

Head stuff ... it ain't gray matter!

We don't have the funding to do a lab analysis on the fuzz, but to us it looked and felt a lot like the stuff that you find when you open a jar of vitamins. Perhaps this is a valiant recycling effort on the part of some habitual vitamin or prescription–drug user that wants to get rid of that cottony stuff without filling the landfills.

Above: The stuff we found inside the head.

Dangerous leisure, son

Remember those hideous polyester leisure suits that plagued us in the '70s? We found them! Careful examination of the inside of the Beanies led us to the startling discovery that the "hide" of the cute little beasts is actually made of recycled polyester leisure suits! Apparently, they found a way to add some fluffy fuzz stuff to the outside to disguise their disposal *(see chapter 3)*.

Above: Close examination reveals that the hide is constructed of recycled polyester leisure suits.

Inside out or evil-side in?

We're sorry that we have to show you this, but we feel that it is of vital importance. Pictured on the right is our Beanie autopsy specimen turned inside out. We couldn't help but notice that this procedure transformed the cute little stuffed plush toy into an evil-looking, bug-eyed, bull-dog-piggish-looking scary thing. Could it be that what we found is really the actual outside of a hideous beast that had been turned inside prior to stuffing? Could it be that each of what people perceive to be normal, cute, fuzzy little stuffed animals are actually hideous little demonic beasts that have managed to transform themselves into cuddly plush toys by turning themselves inside out so they could infiltrate the world and take over our souls?

I digress. This line of thought falls into the realm of a conspiracy theory and we aren't to that chapter yet. Sorry.

Above: No, it's not a creature from a Stephen King novel—it's our Beanie autopsy specimen turned inside out!

Identifying Counterfeits

• •

Insist on the genuine article.

We had heard about the so-called counterfeit Beanies. Granted, if you are going to bother to collect something you ought to make sure that you are collecting the genuine article and not a cheap imitation. And, sure enough, in our careful dissection of over two hundred seemingly "authentic" Beanies, we did discover that a few rip-offs (imposters) had crept into the lot. From outward appearances, they all looked virtually identical. But what we found on the inside could give Geraldo at least two hours of prime-time material. Here then are just a few of the amazing counterfeit Beanies that we found.

Right top: Beanie #142 was filled with jelly beans.

Right bottom: After watching Beanie #205 swell up and turn a golden brown when applying flame, we opened it up to find a mess of mini marshmallows.

NO.142

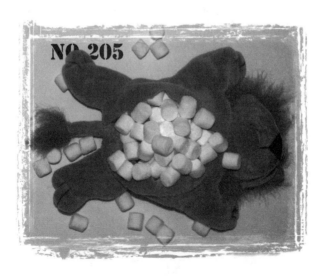

NO. 205

Colombian drug trafficking?

Sorry, this may be jumping the gun on our chapter 3 conspiracy theories a bit, but upon opening Beanie #129, we were surprised to find a half pound of espresso–roast coffee beans! While we found no further evidence of drug trafficking in this Beanie, we couldn't help but remember that *Rockford Files* episode when Jim found cocaine stashed in a shipment of coffee. Or was it Axel Foley in *Beverly Hills Cop*? Whatever, we found it very suspicious.

Note: The beans did lend a pleasant aroma to the toy. This may be a stuffing method that the manufacturers might want to consider when sales start to slump. You could also stuff the wiener dog models with Cuban cigars and get yourself into a whole new market: Guys!

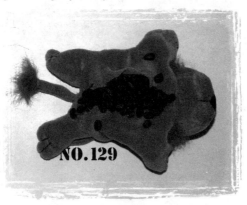

NO.129

Pasta Pets

We thought this one felt kind of funny before we ever ripped it open. Inside we found pasta–penne noodles to be precise. Peculiar yes, but they made one heck of a lunch when we cooked them al denté (Italian for "like rubber bands") and melted a little of the processed cheese found in Beanie #57 over them. If we had only found one filled with a nice marinara sauce . . .

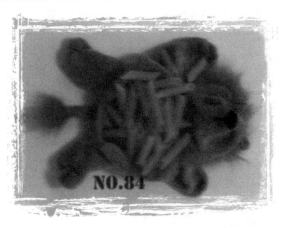

Above: Beanie #84 was probably from Italy. Sorry about the poor quality photo; the steam from the pasta water fogged up our camera lens.

Left: Beanie #129 was filled with a half pound of stale espresso-roast coffee beans.

Rice-a-Beanie

If we'd found a special seasoning packet in it we would assume that #204 was from San Francisco. But the short–grain white rice led us to believe that this counterfeit Beanie was from the Orient.

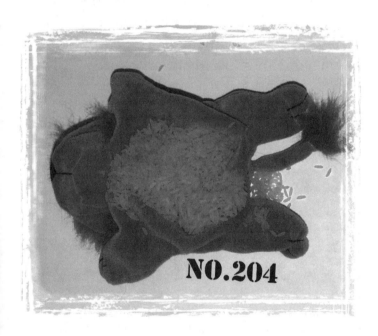

Above: Beanie #204 was filled with rice.

Creating Counterfeits

●●●●●●●●●●●●●●●●●●●●●●●●●●●●●●●

Re-manufacturing for more value

Obviously, counterfeit Beanies are not worth as much as the genuine article. However, we have discovered that manufacturing flaws in the genuine article can actually increase the value of the Beanie.

So, Dr. Al and I took a couple hours at the end of our autopsy session to create what we knew would be a gold mine of "rare manufacturing-flawed Beanies" once we showed them to greedy and unsuspecting collectors!

Don't worry, by the time this book hits the shelves and the collectors find out they've been duped, we'll have skipped the country.

"Tripod" the 3-Legged, 3-Eyed Dog

Cost of original bulldog Beanie $5.95

Cost of extra eye from craft store   .20

Time to make   Twenty minutes

Total cost $6.15

Estimate value if sold as rare defect $5,500.00

Your profit!   ***$5,493.85***

"Cowrab"

Accidental "Surf and Turf!" But surf and turf at your local restaurant never fetched $2,700.00! That's what we sold this one for to a woman in Spangler, Ohio, who told us that she would use her expected profits to pay for her son's entire college tuition! This much fun should be outlawed!

"Koalaala" the Siamese Koalas

A lack of "koalaty control" at the Beanie manufacturing plant has led to the rare edition of 100 Siamese koalas! Our cost per set was $11.90. Our asking price will be a mere $1,500.00 per twin set. And our net profit after the sale of all 100 koala twins? *$148,810.00!*

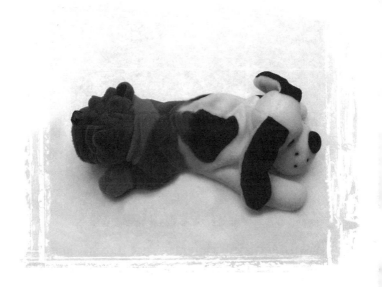

"SpotRover"

No more chasing the tail or sniffing of rears with this creation! We intend to ask $750.00 for each of these cute little duomutts, and $600.00 each for the other version (two rear ends).

"Dual Porpoise"

This manufacturing defect looks like an accident that happened while playing "Chicken of the Sea!" Well, it's no accident that we cleared an easy $15,000 selling twenty of these bad boys!

It's like winning the lottery without having to pick any numbers!

• •

Publisher's note: We do not endorse the unethical activities of "Dr." B. Neebascher and Dr. Al as described in this chapter. If you purchased one of the "rare defect Beanies" please do not contact us to get your money back, and we have no idea where the "doctors" have relocated.

Chapter Three
Beanie Conspiracy Theories

● ●

Collected from "reliable sources"
throughout North America and Guam.

Above: A "Beanie mothership" beaming Beanies to Earth.

Right: The random falling of beans led to the Alien Invasion Theory as submitted by Mrs. Leonard Robb of Cherokee, Iowa.

Alien Invasion   —Mrs. Leonard Robb

As an avid Beanie collector for over four years now, I have had my share of Beanies spill their beans. But none had ever spilled like this!

One Saturday afternoon as I was arranging my Beanie collection for display at my afternoon tea with Alma Erickson, my cat jumped up and grabbed the tie-dye fish Beanie and ripped it open. I yelled, "Scat!" But the damage had already been done. The Beanie was ruined and the beans had fallen onto my carpet.

As I headed to get my vacuum cleaner, I looked at the spill and was astonished to see that the random spill of the beans had formed an alien face!

This remarkable discovery led me to the theory that the little white beads were actually alien eggs waiting to hatch.

I believe to this day that Beanies are being distributed throughout the world and one day will hatch, all at one time, causing an unannounced full-fledged alien invasion of the entire earth! I'm really quite upset!

Polyester Double-Take
—"Dr." B. Neebascher

I briefly described this startling discovery in chapter 2 of my book, *The Official Beanie Basher Handbook* (1998, Andrews McMeel). But I believe it warrants closer examination due to the potentially devastating implications of this discovery.

When turned inside out, the Beanie "hide" revealed itself to be old polyester "double-knit" leisure suits that had been flocked to look like plush and then sewn into the shape of small animals and turned once again into a national craze.

Those of you who are too young to remember the 1970s may not recall the first incarnation of the fabric–a fashion crazy (more accurately, fashion atrocity) called the "Leisure Suit." Men of all ages were duped into purchasing and wearing the synthetic suit under the misguided hope of attaining a wrinkle-free, stain-resistant life of leisure. Instead of providing a leisurely existence, the suits turned us into a nation of dweebs. We were scorned by the rest of the world. The value of our dollar fell to foreign currencies. We lost our senses.

Above: Close examination reveals that the "hide" of the Beanie is actually constructed of what appears to be recycled polyester leisure suits.

We elected an actor to the presidency!

And now, the evil fabric that we thought had long since been retired to live out its half–life in landfills (or at least to live on the backs of retirees in Florida) has once again reared its ugly knit in the form of little Beanie Beasts. And, once again, the whole of America (but primarily women *this* time) is being duped into the false promises of the lurid fabric.

Buyers beware! It's not too late to stop America from repeating a horrible mistake.

Toxic Waste Dump   —Anonymous

I'm not giving out my name with this story so I won't be jeopardizin' the safety of my loved ones when this here book is published. But I swear it's the truth!

I have this on good authority. Jerry down at Mac's Truck Stop told me that Pastor Emil over at the Lutheran Church in Clarkston told him that them little Beanie Buddy thingers is filled with toxic waste from the chemical plant down in Masonville.

You've got to admit that it's a real clever way of disposin' of toxic waste—having folks linin' up to buy the stuff. Sure, it sounds far-fetched. But it must be the truth, cause when I bought my niece one of them things, it made me itch all over. Well, it was either that or there was poison ivy in them woods I was clearin' earlier in the day.

At any rate, I wouldn't put it past some high-buck corporation to come up with the idea. So I ain't buyin' any more of them Beanie Buddies until someone does a white paper report on 'em. I think they're ugly anyhow.

You betcha!

Other Conspiracy Theories
—John and Joan Q. Public

I took my hidden camera to the street to gather more Beanie conspiracy theories. Unfortunately, the camera battery was dead and I was unable to document any of my findings. But here, to my best recollection, are some of the thoughts of average citizens as to the origin and subversive purposes of Beanies:

"They're a communist plot to gain control of the U.S. currency and the movie industry."

Sounds feasible . . . at least it would have sounded feasible back in the '50s.

"Them things is filled with Japanese ant eggs!"

I should note that this person lives next door to Mrs. Leonard Robb.

"Beanies? They're just cute little fluffy toys."

Ya, right!

"They's filled with microchips that's gonna fuse together to transmit our thoughts to the government via that Internetwork thing."

Obviously, Bill Gates has a hand in this phenomenon.

What's your theory?
E-mail it to: beaniebasher@octane.com

39

Chapter Four
Retiring Your Own Beanies

• •

No need to wait until someone tells you that your Beanies have been retired. Just follow these easy hints and you can retire your own Beanies right now!

Bumper Beanies

If your insurance is up-to-date, duct tape your Beanies on your front and rear bumpers. Then enter the demolition derby or enlist the services of a New York taxi.

Bowser's Beanies

Your dog will love to help you "retire" your Beanies. Simply play catch for a while, then tug-of-war for a while, then leave the dog alone with the Beanie retirement project.

Hedging Your Bets

Here is a way to retire multiple Beanies at once. Simply place the Beanies in the teeth of your electric hedge trimmer and plug it in.

Caution: Using this technique may also retire your fingers.

Beanie Lumberjack

If you want to get even more aggressive in your retirement procedures, start up the old chain saw, tape the throttle down, and toss it into a fifty-gallon drum of Beanies.

Caution: It is not advisable to reach into the barrel until the saw has run out of gas.

Drill Press

Your Beanies can retire with a "holier than thou"
attitude when you take the drill press to them.

Re-Tire

Don't have the heart to run them over yourself? Just find a parked delivery truck and wait for the driver to finish his delivery. This is a great method to use when prepping for Beanie wall–paper *(see chapter 5)*.

The Beanie Bash

You probably got your Beanies at a mall, so why not have them retire at the maul? This method of retirement, whether you mash them on an anvil, a boulder, or your driveway, provides a great release for your pent-up anger from having succumbed to the Beanie craze.

Note: This method will leave the hide pretty much intact, allowing for some of the Beanie hide applications found in chapter 5.

A New Angle on Beanie Retirement

Using a power miter box not only does a fine job of dispatching your Beanies, the chopping action also provides a certain satisfaction found previously only when using the maul method.

Cut Your Retirement Time in Half

Halving your Beanies provides twice the side-splitting fun when you gang 'em up on the table saw. Just watch those fingers and wear protective eyeware to save you from flying Beanie pellets!

Note: You might recall that we turned this retirement project into some extra cash *(See page 31)*.

The Ultimate Roadkill

Wait until the steamroller operator takes a break then line up your Beanie collection under the roller. The freshly flattened Beanies can then be recruited for any number of alternative uses as described in the next chapter.

Mow'em Down

Line 'em up and mow 'em down! Works equally well with a bagger or mulching blade. What a great way to get your teenage son to mow the lawn!

Beanie Chipper

It worked for that guy in the *Fargo* movie, and it'll work for your entire Beanie collection.

Note: The resultant "Beanie chips" make a great mulch for your garden. (For other recycling hints, see the next chapter.)

Publisher's note: Implementing any of "Dr." Neebascher's sick techniques may result in personal injury, imprisonment, or both. We suggest that you ignore this entire chapter and skip right to chapter 5 for the socially and environmentally responsible means of recycling your Beanie collection.

Retire with a Railroad Pension

My personal favorite method is that of retiring an entire Beanie collection in one pass of a loco-motive. Simply line up your Beanies on the track and wait for a passing freight train. Maybe it's a carryover from my youthful practice of flatten-ing pennies on the railroad track. Maybe I just like trains....

Just make sure you are well away from the track when the train comes. And if the train derails, you have never heard of "Dr." B. Neebascher or this book.

• •

Whichever method you select to retire your Beanies, whether it's one of ours or one from your own sick mind, you must remember to practice the com-monsense safety precautions your high school shop teacher taught you and always wear the proper eye protection.

Chapter Five
Alternative Uses for Beanies

● ●

You may feel like donating your entire Beanie collection to your local refuse service once you come to realize that you've been duped.
STOP!
Restrain yourself!
There are obviously plenty more environmentally and socially responsible uses for your collection than dumping them in the local landfill!

Put your Beanies to work for you by implementing these clever ideas.

Beanie Draft Damper

Your Beanies make great insulation against winter breezes that sneak in under doors and around windows.

• •

Packaging Material

Shipping your breakables is a breeze with Beanies! Just pack them around your valuables, seal the box, and ship away!

Bonus Hint: Throw in an extra copy of *The Official Beanie Basher Handbook* and the recipient of the box can employ any of these clever Beanie recycling ideas themselves.

Beanie Airbag

Car not equipped with an airbag? This idea is probably safer than having 300 pounds of bag thrust into your face. Just epoxy an assortment of Beanies to your steering wheel.

Beanie-Top Car

The vinyl roof of the '70s has nothing on this baby! Epoxy a colorful assortment of Beanies on your roof and you'll be the talk of the strip.

On second thought, why stop with the roof? If your collection is large enough, glue 'em all over your entire vehicle!

The Mower-Toss Game

Here's an adaptation of the old clown-face beanbag toss. Just start up your mower, tip it over as shown, and toss the Beanies into the spinning blade. (Stop the mower before retrieving Beanies.) Hours of fun for the whole family!

Beanie Bedspread

Stitch your Beanie collection to the top of a sheet and you have a colorful and cozy quilt.

Beanie Door-Ding Damper

Glue Beanies on your car door edges to prevent unsightly door-ding damage to neighboring vehicles. It's a very socially responsible thing to do!

Note: If you implemented the full-car coverage hint from page 61, you have already experienced the benefits of this tip.

Beanied Car Seat Cover

Taxicab drivers will like this one. It provides the same comfort as a beaded car seat cover, yet with the warmth of plush.

Beanie Garage Perfect Parker

A strategically placed pile of Beanies to stop
your front wheels means a perfect park every
time you pull into your garage.

Beanie Gas Cap

Lose your gas cap? Never fear! Just cram a Beanie into the hole to prevent gas from evaporating until you replace the cap.

When you do replace the gas cap, the temporary Beanie cap works great as a barbecue coal starter. Just pile the coals on top, toss in a match and step back! (Full fire–fighting gear including an asbestos suite is recommended.) The Beanie adds a nice plastic flavor to your meat.

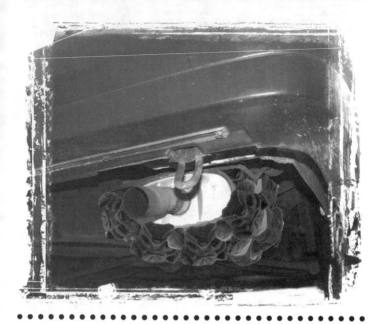

Beanie Muffler

We pretested this one for you and, until it burst into flames, this collection of Beanies glued around our holey muffler really did an admirable job of quieting down the car! However, when you try it, we recommend that you somehow fire-proof your Beanies first.

Beanie Wallpaper

Sure it looks hideous, but it *is* a step up from the old flocked wallpaper that used to be here. Glue your Beanie "hides" or fully beaned Beanies to your walls to prevent damage when you're bouncing off the walls from cabin fever.

Beanies Home on the Range

Forget the bucket of golf balls. Bring a bucket of Beanies to use at the driving range. I found that the appendages made it particularly easy to correct my habitual slice. It's a great way to introduce kids to golf, too!

Beanie Boat Bumpers

Be the envy of the lake crowd when your boat is adorned with these adorable plush boat bumpers. And get the kids to wear those life preservers by covering them with stitched-on Beanies.

• •

Stucco Replacement

Tired of your plain old stucco siding? Side your house with your Beanie collection using any industrial-strength, weatherproof adhesive.

Note: The house above is a work in progress. The owner is seeing if the adhesive stands up to the rain before he covers the entire house. So far so good.

Beanie Landfill

Bothered by pesky sinkholes in your backyard? If not, I'll bet plenty of your neighbors would appreciate your help filling theirs. And nothing says "landfill" better than your retired Beanie collection!

Beanie Golf

If you've become a scratch player at your local mini-golf course, you can increase the challenge by littering each hole with Beanies.

Beanie Pothole Repair

Donation of your Beanie collection to your local highway department won't only garner you a nice tax write-off (especially if you claim them at their full projected retirement value*), but it will help fill and smooth those aggravating potholes with a nondegradable and durable filler.

*Consult your tax professional for deductibility information. I'm just guessing here.

Shopping Cart Bumpers

Curb damage from runaway shopping carts. Epoxy four or five Beanies to each of the front corners of your shopping cart. Fix a new cart each time you shop. The store owner will love you for it and so will the store's insurance agent.

● ●

Popeye Beanie Vise Game

Entertain the kids for hours!

1) Put a Beanie in the vise.

2) Contestants take turns tightening the handle.

3) The contestant whose handle turn pops out
   the eyes of the Beanie wins.

• •
Beanie Traction

When the snow is flying, keep a few dozen Beanies in your trunk in case you get stuck. If you get stuck, the Beanies won't work quite as well as sand, but they aren't as messy as using actual roadkill for providing extra traction.

Beanie Free Throw

Line up your Beanies for temporary court markings. They do a nice job of tripping up the competition, thus creating the ultimate in home-court advantage.

Beanie Bikeseat Buffer

Pad those uncomfortably hard bike seats by hot–gluing a few Beanies in the appropriate areas of the seat and you'll be sittin' pretty and comfy.

● ●
Handle Beanies

Don't stop at the seat; tape some Beanies onto your handlegrips to lessen the hammering that your hands and wrists take while riding.

Shady Beanies

Fix torn lamp shades by gluing full Beanies or their "hides" to the lamp shade frame. Sure, it looks hideous, but so did that old shade.

Beanie Privacy Fence

Turn your see-through cyclone fencing into a colorful privacy fence by stuffing the holes with your Beanie collection. If your fence borders the neighbor's property, you can choose to show them the heads or tails (depending on what kind of terms you are on).

Beanie Mulch

Adding a Beanie mulch around tree seedlings helps retain moisture and discourages pests.

Beanie Stool Cushions

Easily convert hard wooden bar stools into soft, cushiony seats with an assortment of Beanies adhered with wood glue.

Beanieburger

Here's a practical joke you can play when you want to be taken out to dinner:

Prepare a Beanie "burger" plate as shown above and set it before your significant other. After you both have a hearty, knee–slapping laugh, put on your coat 'cause you're goin' out for dinner!

• •

Beanies up the Tailpipe

Speaking of practical jokes ...

Stuff some Beanies into the tailpipe of the local road hog. Then challenge him to a drag race down at the strip. The back pressure on the engine will kill his efforts and at the same time rid you of a few Beanies.

Beanie Roofing

Get out your pneumatic nailer and get ready for an afternoon of fun as you reroof your house in Beanies! It will provide extra warmth in the winter and added protection if you live in an area plagued by hail storms.

Skeptical of Beanies' durability as shingles? Do like I did: start with your garage–it's the perfect companion for your Beanie-top car *(see page 61)*.

Beanie Stoll

It's not politically correct to wear real animal fur anymore. But, thus far, no one has complained about wearing stuffed-animal fur. So, fashion a lovely Beanie "fur" collar. Or, depending on the size of your collection, an entire Beanie coat.

Beanie Club Covers

Cut a horizontal slit between your Beanies' hind legs and they'll fit nicely over your putter and irons as club covers. Too bad there's a fourteen–club limit! That's okay–just make sets for your golfing buddies, too!

Beanie-Padded Toilet Seat

I can't think of a more appropriate application of these furry little guys than rallying the troops to create a colorful Beanie-padded toilet seat.

Beanie Eyeglass Case

A Beanie tracheotomy (a simple slit at the neck–line) can turn any Beanie you desire into a soft eyeglass case for your reading glasses. Or, glue the converted Beanie to your car visor to hold your sunglasses.

Beanie Mud Flaps

A strong epoxy holds Beanies to your wheel–wells creating plush mud flaps for your vehicle.

Soap Dish

Any Beanie (but preferably one with four legs) becomes a soft sink-side companion that holds your slimy bar soap. You can use it to scrub out the sink once a month, too.

Mop Head Replacement

Two or three Beanies attached to your favorite mop handle will do a nice job of washing and waxing your floors.

Beanie Hot Pads

Use Beanies to remove hot casserole dishes from the oven, then enlist the services of four Beanies to protect your table from the blazing heat of the dish.

Beanie Duster

A spray of furniture polish on the belly of the Beanie beast and you've got a wonderful buffing buddy! Works great with car wax, too!

97

Beanie Beer Holder

Stitch two Beanies (any variety) snout to rear to form a circle in which to slide your favorite canned beverage. Keeps the beverage cool and your hands warm.

Beanie Tub Plug

Lose your bathtub drain plug? Just stuff it with a
Beanie.

Hide Your Valuables

What better place to hide your valuables than in a place of absolutely no interest to a burglar! Slit open the neck of your Beanie, remove the guts, then fill it with your valuable jewelry.

It should be obvious by now that Beanies really can be contributing members of society. You just have to look at them creatively. Before we set you loose, here are a few more alternative Beanie uses to get your creative juices flowing:

• Beanie window coverings (glue on old window shade)
• Prop up legs of wobbly furniture
• Remote control cover (slit, empty, and slide over remote)
• Beanie insoles (stuff into shoes for cushioned walk)
• Beanie-hide picture frame cover for the kiddies' room
• Beanied fireworks (tape to rocket and launch)
• Butt, breast, or spine enhancers–stuff and strut
• Beanie ammunition for mini-pillow fights
• Beanie-lump mattress for unwanted overnight guests
• Beanie biceps (fake under-shirt muscles)
• Beanie padding for any sport
• Beanie blindfold eye covering for mind-reading act
• Beanie Hair Club for Men (just glue onto scalp)
• Beanie kneelers for roofing technicians
• Glue to sharp corners of overhead cupboards
• Fill with cement and use as doorstop
• Beanie pin cushion

There will never be a shortage of Beanies–and what to do with them is limited only by your imagination!

Notes:

This space has been provided to you (at no extra expense) so you can jot down your own ideas for recycling your Beanie collection.

Epilogue
Parting Comments

●●●●●●●●●●●●●●●●●●●●●●●●●●●●●●●●

That's it for now except for this epilogue (no relation to Epilady hair remover). If you are a Beanie addict, I hope that my startling discoveries, hints, and techniques have helped you come to your senses and will be of assistance to you throughout Beanie withdrawal and reprogramming.

If you are like me (and I know *I* am), and your spouse did something stupid like withdrawing your entire retirement savings to "invest in Beanie futures"–well, you'll need more than this little book and your anger support group. You'll need a part–time job bagging groceries well into your golden years. But that's okay. Just remember, you came into this world empty–handed, and you're going to go out that way. So, if hoarding small stuffed animals gives you some sort of satisfaction, go for it! But, if bashing, slicing, dicing, grinding, drilling, sawing, mulching, shredding, stomping, grilling, exploding, julienning, composting, shooting, gashing, mashing, clubbing, stir-frying, blasting, flushing, nuking, torching, nailing, screwing, ripping, rasping, tearing, beating, souffléing, punching, taping, plastering, paving, tarring, feathering, dragging, sanding, buffing, lacquering, dousing in gasoline, and igniting the little buggers gives you pleasure—well, I know how you feel.

—"Dr." B. Neebascher

• •

www.octane.com/beaniebasher

Want to submit some of your own alternative uses for Beanies, or send us love (or hate) mail? Just visit our web site!

We'll selectively post your insights and insanity for the entire world to see.